The Earth's Resources

Rebecca Harman

www.heinemann.co.uk/library

Visit our website to find out more information about Heinemann Library books.

To order:

 Phone 44 (0) 1865 888066

Send a fax to 44 (0) 1865 314091

 Visit the Heinemann Bookshop at www.heinemann.co.uk/library to browse our catalogue and order online.

First published in Great Britain by Heinemann Library, Halley Court, Jordan Hill, Oxford OX2 8EJ, part of Harcourt Education. Heinemann is a registered trademark of Harcourt Education Ltd.

© Harcourt Education Ltd 2005
The moral right of the proprietor has been asserted.

Editorial: Melanie Copland
Design: Victoria Bevan and AMR Design
Illustration: Art Construction and David Woodroffe
Picture Research: Mica Brancic and Helen Reilly
Production: Duncan Gilbert

Originated by Chroma Graphics (Overseas) Pte. Ltd
Printed in China by WKT Company Limited

The paper used to print this book comes from sustainable resources.

ISBN 0 431 01302 0
09 08 07 06 05
10 9 8 7 6 5 4 3 2 1

British Library Cataloguing in Publication Data
Harman, Rebecca
The Earth's Resources; renewable and non-renewable (Earth's Processes)
333.7'9
A full catalogue record for this book is available from the British Library.

Acknowledgements
The Publishers would like to thank the following for permission to reproduce photographs: Alamy Images/Stan Kujawa **p.14**; Corbis **pp. 4**, **6**, **12**, **13**, **19**, **22**, **26**; Corbis/William McNamee **p.5**; Corbis/Cordaiy Photo Library **p.25**, Corbis/Peter Beck **p.27**; Corbis/Terry W Eggers **p.8**; Creatas **p.23**; Digital Vision **pp. 24, 28**; Getty Images/Stone **p.7**; Getty Images/Stone **p.9**; Getty Images/AFP **p.20**; Getty Images/PhotoDisc **p.21**; Science Photo Library **p.17**; Still Pictures/Frischmuth **p.11**; Still Pictures/Al Grillo **p.16**.

Cover photograph of a slag heap at the Nan Helen opencast coal mine at Coelbren, Wales, UK reproduced with permission of Corbis/Ecoscene/Chinch Gryniewicz.

The Publishers would like to thank Nick Lapthorn for his assistance in the preparation of this book.

Contents

Words appearing in the text in bold, like this, are explained in the Glossary.

What are the Earth's resources?

From the moment you get up in the morning to the moment you go to bed you use the Earth's **resources**. All over the world people make use of resources to provide the things they need in their everyday lives.

Did you know?

When you wash using hot water, when you eat your breakfast, when you watch TV, and when you turn on a light you are using the Earth's resources.

A resource is something that is useful to us. The Earth's resources are natural and are found everywhere; on land, in the oceans, in the sky, and deep underground. The Earth is full of resources, but they are not always found in the places where they are needed, so they have to be sent around the world.

The Earth's resources are being used to light up the city of Hong Kong in China.

Examples of important resources include water and **energy**. If water did not fall to the ground as rain, plants would not grow. There would be nothing for animals to eat, and we would have no plants or animals to eat. Without water we would not exist, in fact, there would be no life on Earth at all.

The main energy resources we use for heating and lighting in our homes are **coal**, **oil**, and **natural gas**. These are found deep underground or deep under the ocean. In this book we will be looking in detail at the Earth's energy resources.

Did you know?

We call gas that comes from the Earth "natural gas".

These men are drilling for oil. Oil is used to make petrol which we need to drive our cars.

Resources are split into two types: non-renewable and renewable.

- **Non-renewable resources**, such as coal, oil, and natural gas, take millions of years to form. They will eventually run out.

- **Renewable resources**, such as the Sun and the wind, can be used over and over again and will not run out.

We use resources every day, and everyone in the world depends on them. As the world's population grows, more people will be using these natural resources. Many of the Earth's resources are now being used up faster than nature can replace them.

The Sun's energy can be trapped at solar power stations like this one in California in the United States.

How are energy resources used?

The Earth's energy resources are being used very quickly. This is causing concern to many people. As the world's population grows, more and more people need energy resources for travelling by car, bus, train, or aeroplane. We also need energy for cooking, heating, and lighting, and for making things like televisions and washing machines work.

Most of the energy used by machines is in the form of **electricity**. The Earth's resources are used to make electricity in places called power stations. Most power stations use non-renewable resources such as coal, oil, and natural gas to produce electricity. Some use renewable resources such as the Sun.

The Earth's resources are used to produce electricity in power stations.

In power stations the Earth's resources are used to create heat, which is then used to heat up water. When the water heats up, steam is produced, just like steam is produced when you boil a kettle at home. This steam is then used to make machines called **turbines** produce electricity. A turbine is like a windmill, and the steam makes the blades turn. The electricity then travels along cables to wherever it is needed, such as homes, schools, shopping centres, and factories.

Did you know?

One-quarter of the world's population lives in rich countries such as the United States, the United Kingdom, and Australia. These people use three-quarters of the Earth's energy resources.

Electricity travels along cables to the places where it is needed.

What are non-renewable resources?

Non-renewable resources are those that have a limited supply on Earth. These resources are being taken from the Earth and used up much quicker than they are being replaced. This means they will eventually run out.

Fossil fuels are non-renewable resources and include coal, oil, and natural gas. They are the most important energy resource on Earth today. They supply around 90 per cent of the energy we use for running our cars and making electricity.

Fossil fuels form over millions of years from the remains of dead plants and animals. When they are burned, energy is released as heat and light.

Did you know?

It took nature one million years to create the amount of fossil fuel being burned on Earth today in one year.

All of these cars are using fossil fuels.

What is coal?

Coalfields are the remains of huge forests that existed millions of years ago when the Earth was much warmer and wetter than it is now. Coal is formed from the dead remains of these forests. When the forest plants and trees died, they fell to the swampy forest floor and were covered with layers of sediment (sand and mud). Over millions of years, as the remains were buried deeper under more and more layers of sediment, they became squashed and turned into coal.

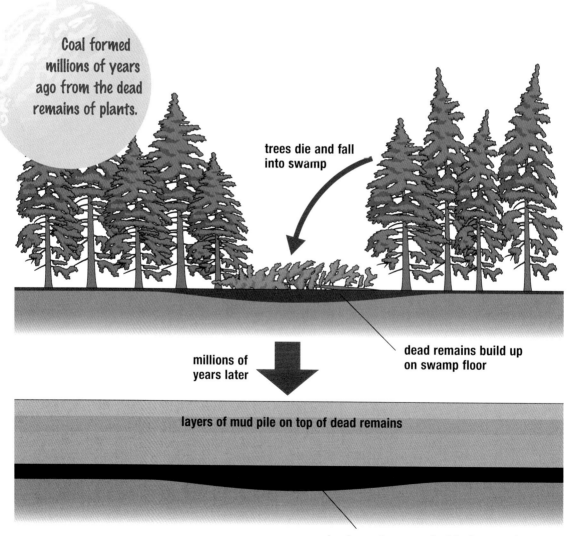

Coal formed millions of years ago from the dead remains of plants.

trees die and fall into swamp

millions of years later

dead remains build up on swamp floor

layers of mud pile on top of dead remains

dead remains squashed to form coal

Coal is buried underground, so it needs to be **extracted** by mining. Mining is a way of extracting resources by blasting rocks and digging tunnels underground. The coal can then be burned in power stations to produce electricity, or used for heating homes in coal fires.

Coal is mined in countries such as the United Kingdom, Germany, Russia, China, Australia, and the United States. Before the discovery of oil, coal was the most important energy resource on Earth. Now it has mostly been replaced by oil and natural gas, so many coal mines have been closed.

Coal is often buried beneath hundreds of metres of rock and has to be mined to extract it from the Earth.

What are oil and natural gas?

Oil is now the world's most important energy resource, supplying 40 per cent of the world's energy. It is necessary for modern life, as it is used for petrol, aeroplane fuel, and heating. It can also be used to make plastics, soap, paint, and glue. Natural gas supplies 20 per cent of the world's energy. Together oil and natural gas provide twice as much energy as coal.

Oil and natural gas are formed from the dead remains of plants and animals. Millions of years ago, tiny sea creatures and plants died, fell to the ocean floor and became covered with layers of sediment. As the remains were buried deeper under more layers of sediment, they became squashed and eventually turned into oil and gas.

Oil rigs are platforms built for drilling down into the ocean floor to extract oil and natural gas.

Because oil is a liquid, it seeps up through cracks and holes in the rocks. It does this until it is trapped by a layer of rock it cannot pass through, called **impermeable rock**. Scientists need to find these **oil traps** so that they can drill deep into the ground and release the oil. Gas also collects in traps, sometimes with oil and sometimes on its own.

Once the oil and gas have been collected, they are moved to places called **oil refineries** by oil tankers or pipelines. Here they are made into petrol and the other forms of oil that we can use.

Did you know?

The largest **oil reserves** are found in Saudi Arabia in the Middle East. The largest natural gas reserves are found in Russia.

This pipeline in Alaska is used to carry oil to oil refineries.

What are the problems with fossil fuels?

We extract billions of tonnes of coal, billions of barrels of oil, and trillions of litres of natural gas from the Earth each year! These fossil fuels took millions of years to form, and are being used up very quickly – much faster than they are being replaced. Sooner or later, there will not be much left.

When fossil fuels are burned, they release harmful gases into the air. Power stations release a gas called sulphur dioxide, and car exhausts release a gas called nitrogen dioxide. These gases dissolve in rainwater to form **acid rain**. When the acid rain falls into lakes and rivers it kills the fish and plants. It also kills many trees and damages buildings as it makes the stone crumble.

These trees in Poland have been killed by acid rain.

Did you know?

Scientists think that the Earth's reserves of oil will last for 40 years, gas will last for 60 years, and coal will last for 250 years. After these lengths of time, they will be gone forever.

Fossil fuels also give off a gas called carbon dioxide when they are burned. Because of the huge use of fossil fuels over the last 200 years, the amount of carbon dioxide in the air has increased. Carbon dioxide is a **greenhouse gas**. This means that it traps some of the Earth's outgoing heat, like the glass roof of a greenhouse. As the amount of carbon dioxide in the air increases, it traps more heat, and so the Earth gets warmer. This is called the **greenhouse effect**. If the Earth gets warmer, the ice at the North and South Pole could melt, causing sea levels to rise by 1.5 metres. This is called **global warming**.

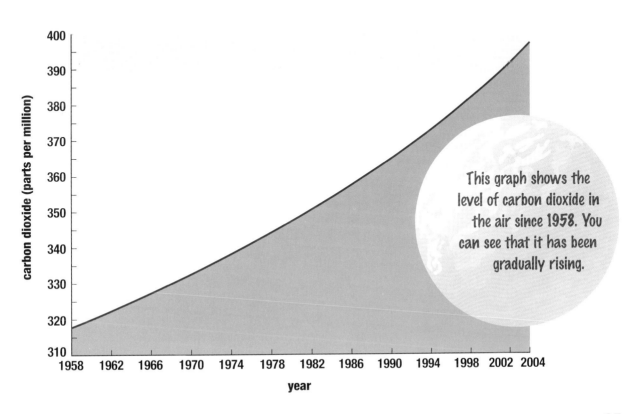

This graph shows the level of carbon dioxide in the air since 1958. You can see that it has been gradually rising.

If fossil fuels are not moved carefully, spillages can occur, causing **pollution** in the ocean or on land. If an oil tanker has an accident, oil may escape into the ocean, killing fish and birds. In 1999 an oil tanker called *Erika* broke apart in the ocean near the north-west coast of France. It spilled more than 10 million litres (3 million gallons) of oil, killing as many as 100,000 seabirds.

Did you know?

The largest oil spill in the United States happened in 1989, when an oil tanker called the *Exxon Valdez* ran aground in southern Alaska, and spilled 49 million litres (10.8 million gallons) of oil. This is enough oil to fill 125 Olympic-sized swimming pools.

A bird killed by an oil spillage from the tanker *Exxon Valdez*.

What is nuclear power?

Because of all the problems with fossil fuels, we need to find other energy resources. Some scientists think that **nuclear power** is cleaner and safer than fossil fuels. Nuclear power is another non-renewable resource.

Nuclear power stations use a **radioactive** mineral called **uranium**. Uranium is mined from deep underground in countries such as Canada, the United States, South Africa, Namibia, France, and Australia. In nuclear power stations the uranium is not burned, like we burn fossil fuels. Instead the uranium **particles** are split into smaller particles. This is called a **nuclear reaction**. This reaction releases a lot of energy which can then be used to create electricity.

Although nuclear power is a non-renewable resource, only a tiny amount of uranium is needed in power stations, as it is very powerful. This means there is little chance that all of the uranium in the world will be used up.

In this nuclear power station, you can see radioactive parts being stored under water until they can be buried in concrete.

From the information so far, you may think that nuclear power is the perfect answer to the problems of fossil fuels. But there is one major problem with nuclear power. It produces very dangerous radioactive waste material. This waste is dangerous to people and animals. It has to be buried in thick concrete containers deep underground.

If there is an accident in a nuclear power station, there is a danger that radioactivity will be released into the surrounding area. In 1986, a huge cloud of radioactive material escaped from the Chernobyl nuclear power station in the Ukraine. The high radiation levels killed more than 30 people immediately, and 135,000 people had to be moved out of the area.

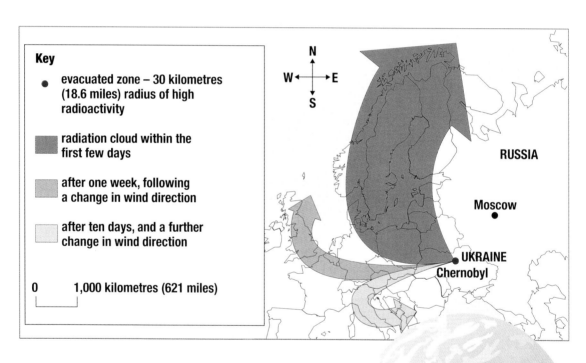

Key

- evacuated zone – 30 kilometres (18.6 miles) radius of high radioactivity

- radiation cloud within the first few days

- after one week, following a change in wind direction

- after ten days, and a further change in wind direction

0   1,000 kilometres (621 miles)

N
W ← → E
S

RUSSIA

Moscow

UKRAINE
Chernobyl

Did you know?

Just 100 grams (3.5 ounces) of uranium produces as much energy as 1 tonne of coal.

The disaster at Chernobyl affected people over a huge area. Winds carried the radioactive particles all over Europe, ruining crops and affecting food supplies.

What are renewable resources?

The problems with non-renewable resources mean that we should try to find other energy resources we can use.

The Earth has many natural resources available. Some of these resources, such as the Sun and the wind, exist in unlimited supplies. These are called renewable resources, as we can use them again and again and they will not run out.

Did you know?

As long ago as 200 BC, people in China and the Middle East used windmills to pump water and grind grain.

Scientists have discovered ways of using the power from these resources to make electricity. This is good news because renewable resources will give us supplies of energy that we can go on using forever. Another good thing about renewable resources is that they do not pollute the environment like fossil fuels.

The Sun's energy is a renewable resource.

At the moment, these energy sources only provide about 10 per cent of our energy needs (compared with 90 per cent for fossil fuels). Scientists need to work out how these renewable energy resources can supply enough energy to replace fossil fuels in the future.

What is solar power?

Solar power is the name we give to the power of the Sun. The Sun's rays can be captured using **solar panels** on the roofs of buildings, and the energy collected can be used to heat water. The Sun's rays can also be turned into electricity using solar cells, called **photovoltaic cells**, like the ones on a solar powered calculator. One of the largest solar power stations in the world is in French Polynesia, in the Pacific Ocean. Here, 2,000 photovoltaic cells provide enough electricity for homes, schools, hospitals, and street lights.

Solar panels trap energy from the Sun. That energy can be used to heat water.

The Sun does not get used up when it is turned into electricity – it will continue to shine. Getting energy from solar power works best in countries like Australia that have a lot of sunshine. But it also works in less sunny countries like the United Kingdom, as the energy can be stored and used on days when it is not sunny.

This solar powered calculator has tiny solar cells.

solar cells

What is wind power?

The movement of the wind can be used to turn the blades of a **wind turbine**. A wind turbine is similar to a windmill, but the blades look like aeroplane wings. The turbines turn the movement of the blades into electricity. To make enough electricity for a town, lots of wind turbines are needed. A place with lots of turbines is called a **wind farm**. One wind farm in California has 18,000 wind turbines.

This method can only produce energy when the wind is blowing, so it cannot supply electricity all the time. Some people do not like wind farms as they make a lot of noise and spoil the natural landscape.

Some people think wind farms are ugly. What do you think?

Did you know?

The largest wind turbines are over 100 metres (328 feet) tall and their blades can turn at 400 kilometres (249 miles) per hour.

What is hydroelectric power?

Hydroelectric power stations use the power of falling water to make electricity. Rainwater is collected in a **reservoir** behind a **dam** high in the mountains. The water is stored there until the energy is needed. Then, doors in the dam are opened, and the water rushes down the mountain in pipes. There are turbines inside these pipes that turn the power of the falling water into electricity.

This method provides most of the electricity needed in countries like Norway and parts of Canada. It works well in these countries because they have lots of mountains and lots of rain.

Did you know?

The dam at the Grand Coulee hydroelectric power station in Washington state in the United States is over 1.6 kilometres (1 mile) long. It is more than twice as tall as Niagara Falls.

The Glen Canyon Dam in Arizona in the United States. After this was built it took about 15 years for Lake Powell to fill up behind it!

How can the ocean produce electricity?

If you have ever been to the ocean, you will know how powerful waves can be. This power can be used to produce electricity.

You may have also noticed how **tides** move up and down the beach. This tidal energy can be captured by trapping water behind a dam at high tide, and then releasing the water through gates in the dam at low tide. This movement of the water can be used to produce electricity. Tidal power stations have been built in countries such as France, Russia, and China.

Wave and tidal power are not used much today as they need a huge area of ocean to produce only a small amount of electricity.

The power of waves can be used to produce electricity.

What is geothermal power?

In some areas of the Earth, such as in Iceland, New Zealand, and Japan, hot rocks beneath the ground can be used to heat water and produce electricity. This is called **geothermal power**. In some places the hot water rises to the surface through cracks in rocks to form geysers and hot springs. A geyser spurts hot water and steam into the air. In other places it needs to be brought to the surface by drilling deep wells. This is very expensive.

The water in this lake in Iceland is hot because it has been heated by hot rocks underground.

How can we use fewer non-renewable resources?

The world's population is growing and we are using more and more of the Earth's non-renewable resources. One day these resources will run out. We need to use less of these non-renewable resources, and make more use of renewable resources.

Every time you switch on a light, a computer, or an air conditioner, you are using electricity. Most electricity is produced by burning fossil fuels. If we all use less electricity, for example, by switching things off when they are not needed, this will save fossil fuels.

A good way to save electricity is to switch lights off when we leave a room.

Many of the things we throw away could be used again or **recycled**. We should try to recycle everything we can. This includes things like glass, tins, cans, and some plastics.

Scientists in some countries have come up with other new resources to reduce our use of fossil fuels. For example, sugar cane alcohol is used instead of petrol in Brazil.

Did you know?

About 40 per cent of cars in Sao Paulo, Brazil use sugar cane alcohol instead of petrol.

You can help to save resources by recycling materials.

Conclusion

The Earth is rich in natural **resources**. They are found on land, in the oceans, and deep underground. All over the world people make use of the Earth's resources to provide the things they need in their everyday lives.

Resources can be sorted into two types – non-renewable and renewable.

Non-renewable resources are available in a limited supply on Earth. They include coal, oil, and natural gas, which take millions of years to form. We all depend on non-renewable resources. As the world's population grows, many of these resources are being used up faster than nature can replace them. They will eventually run out.

Renewable resources, such as the Sun and the wind, exist on Earth in unlimited supplies. They can be used over and over again and will not run out. We need to make more use of these renewable resources and use fewer non-renewable resources. Now you understand more about the Earth's resources, you can help to do this!

A huge oil platform in the North Sea

Fact file

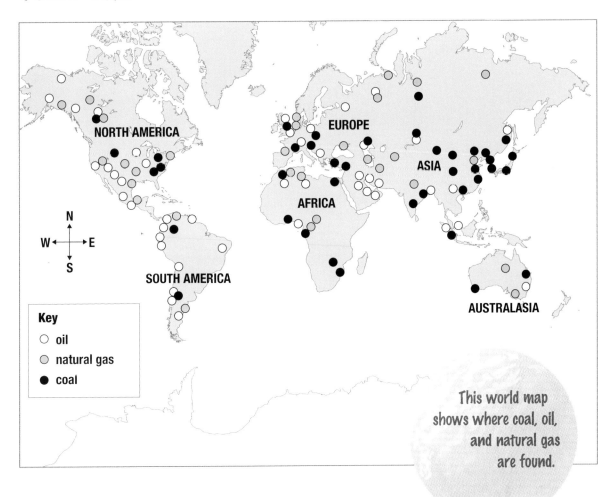

Key
- ○ oil
- ◔ natural gas
- ● coal

This world map shows where coal, oil, and natural gas are found.

Did you know?

- Natural gas was discovered by ancient peoples. The ancient Chinese used natural gas as fuel to boil salty water. They wanted the salt that was left behind after the water had boiled away.

- Coal miners used to take birds underground with them. Poisonous gas in the mines would quickly affect the birds and this would warn the miners, giving them more time to escape.

Glossary

acid rain rain water that has been polluted. It kills plants and wears away buildings

coal dead remains of forest plants, squashed and hardened over millions of years

coalfield area where large reserves of coal are found

dam barrier built across a river to hold back water in a reservoir

electricity energy used by machines

energy power that is used to provide heat

extract take from the ground

fossil fuel fossilized remains of plants and animals that are millions of years old such as coal, oil, and natural gas

geothermal power hot rocks beneath the ground used to heat water and produce electricity

global warming heating up of the Earth

greenhouse effect when the amount of carbon dioxide in the air increases, trapping more heat, and warming up the Earth

greenhouse gas gas such as carbon dioxide that traps some of the Earth's outgoing heat (like the glass roof of a greenhouse)

hydroelectricity electricity produced by the power of falling water

impermeable rock rock that does not have spaces to allow oil or natural gas to seep through

natural gas dead remains of plants and animals on the ocean floor, squashed over millions of years

non-renewable resource resource that will eventually be used up

nuclear power non-renewable energy resource that splits uranium particles to produce energy

nuclear reaction splitting uranium particles into smaller particles to release energy

oil dead remains of plants and animals on the ocean floor, squashed over millions of years

oil refinery place where oil is changed into petrol and other forms that we can use

oil reserve amount of oil in a certain place, which can be extracted

oil trap layer of impermeable rock that oil and natural gas cannot pass through

particle tiny part of something

photovoltaic cell battery that can convert the Sun's energy into electricity

pollution things that are harmful to the environment, for example, car exhaust fumes

radioactive when something contains a type of energy called radiation that is harmful to people

recycle re-use

renewable resource resource that can be used over and over again and will not run out

reservoir lake used for storing water

resource something that is useful to us. The Earth's resources are natural resources

solar panel panel placed on the roof to collect the Sun's energy

solar power energy provided by the Sun

tide movement of sea water up and down the beach

turbine machine like a windmill that produces electricity

uranium radioactive mineral used in nuclear power stations

wind farm lots of wind turbines in one place

wind turbine machine like a windmill that uses the power of the wind to produce electricity

Index

More books to read

Earth Alert: Energy, Jane Featherstone (Hodder Wayland, 2001)
Earth's Precious Resources: Fossil Fuels, Ian Graham (Heinemann Library, 2004)
Green Files: Climate in Crisis, Steve Parker (Heinemann Library, 2003)

Titles in *The Earth's Processes* series include:

Hardback   0 431 01298 9

Hardback   0 431 01299 7

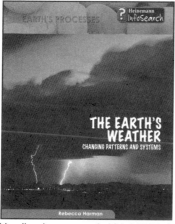

Hardback   0 431 01300 4

Hardback   0 431 01301 2

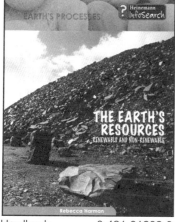

Hardback   0 431 01302 0

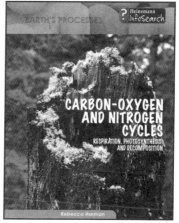

Hardback   0 431 01303 9

Find out about other titles from Heinemann Library on our website www.heinemann.co.uk/library